Provence

PROSPECTS IN COLOR

Provence

FRANCE n⁰ **8**

TEXT
by
MARIE MAURON

•

PHOTOGRAPHS
by
Georges Trubert • Ervin Marton • Atziger
Jacques Fronval • Denis Brihat • Giraudon
Delmas • Roland Gay • Kammermann
Machatschek • Roger Perrin • Photo-Spirale
Pierre Tétrel • Doumic • Féher • Patrice
Molinard • Janine Niepce • Actualit-Rapho
Le Cuziat-Rapho • Robert Thuillier • Yan

TUDOR PUBLISHING COMPANY - NEW YORK

THERE is an old Provençal legend I always love to retell. It goes like this: after God had created the sun, the earth, the mountains and the streams, to His amazement He found He was still left with some of each of these ingredients. What was He to do with these left-overs now? Were these precious materials simply to go to waste? He decided it would be wiser to use them to make a composite of all He had made and which would be His own paradise.

And thus was many-splendoured Provence born, under the charmed smile of the Creator.

★

This legend like most is, of course, an exaggeration, but it does contain a grain of truth. Provence is a true miniature, as varied and complete as the cosmic whole. It owes its diversity, its harmonious and complementary contrasts to the triple influence of the Sea, the Alps and the Rhone. From the mountainous slopes of the province of Dauphiné, Provence opens out and sends the waters of the Rhone rushing, lusting over the plain until, at its delta, it becomes one with the blue Mediterranean.

The Sea is the original Provençal theme which each region varies and enlarges upon in its own manner. And so we have several Provences which, taken together, form the Master Provence which I call ONE in its diversity.

The countryside, the very air and the light in which it bathes, are more virile in what is known as Haute-Provence, balmier on the Riviera, swept by that violent and cold north-west wind known as the mistral in the Rhone valley, and, in the fertile plains, bordered by gently rolling hills, scented with flowering thyme and ripening peaches.

This countryside, atmosphere and light, so typical in one region, become sharp and biting as we near Mont-Ventoux and the Lure mountain chain which, combining in successive tiers with the Alps at Barcelonnette, enclose this vast circle to the north-east.

Geographically, and logically as well, Provence is divided into four regions: the Rhone, the Sea, the mountains and the land. But we in our ramble need not restrict ourselves to visiting each region by itself. Why not, in descending the Rhone, be it by land or water, hop from one bank to the other and back again, touch the neighbouring hills, idle through the plains, make our own routes and look over the sights as our fancy directs?

Several choices are open to us, and it is the river that proposes them all. The river is the royal highway we must

◄ 3 • THE PORTIQUE DE POMPÉE

follow to enter into this joyful kingdom of the sun.

A boat trip down the Rhone from Lyons, where the river becomes navigable, is a thrilling adventure; at every step the countryside becomes a little richer. We join in the vagaries and meanderings of the river itself as it flows through mountain and forest and past perched villages and built up towns.

From Lyons on, it is no longer wild and independent, but, in the style of the true monarch, scatters its wealth about and creates its own cities. Its waters fill with history and overrun with lore. What other valleys, woods and moors, cities and towns, cultivated fields, have seen and felt the onslaught of so many armies and changing civilizations! From the river we see, dotted along its banks, ramparts, ruined chateaux, heroic cities, as we sail down sun-soaked, languorous and magical countryside and by rugged ice and snow-capped mountains.

But now let us leave the river for a while and follow a new venture which comes our way. The town of Bollène, with its enormous Blondel dam. It offers other places of interest: a Roman house, an eleventh century tower, a collegiate dating from the twelfth and seventeenth centuries. Bollène is the gateway to the province of Drôme, which

we enter through the delectable little sun-baked village of Suze-la-Rousse. A detour to the north takes us to the still majestic chateau of Grignan. Another rather charming road leads to Tulette, Saint-Maurice-sur-Aigues, Vinsobres, and finally to Vaison-la-Romaine.

We shall stop here for a while to admire the numerous remains in this former Roman stronghold. Emperor after emperor loved, fortified and adorned it, paid happy visits here and even made it into a capital more powerful than its neighbouring rival city of Avignon. Vaison is a museum. Its very unearthed walls exude history. Most imposing of its sights are the Forum, the Temple of Diana, the Gymnasium, the aqueduct which transported water from the spring of Le Groseau at Malaucène, the magnificent bridge over the Ouvèze, the public and private baths, the arcaded Theatre with its tiers of seats and its stage still intact, the famous Portique de Pompée (Pompey's Gate), the House of the Mesii, and the House of the Dolphin, as it is called, with its outdoor conversation room, and, finally, the perfect remains of the House of the Silver Bust with its beautiful mosaic floors. We can almost feel the bustle of that Greek influenced Roman life as we wander through the roofed street lined

9

LE BARROUX ▲ 7

with shops and adorned with columns. The museum of Vaison is, naturally, one of the richest in France in Greek and particularly Gallo-Roman remains. The centuries which followed continued to add to these riches, and have left us the cathedral of Notre-Dame-de-Nazareth, a perfect example of the Provençal Romanesque style, and a Merovingian church of Saint Quenin with its curious triangular apse and fluted columns. The upper town, built on a rock on the other side of

the famous Roman bridge, is dominated by the imposing ruins of its chateau. This is a charming and picturesque town with its towers, its thick walls, its loop-holes, its pointed cathedral and, also, the captivating charm of its winding streets and pathways.

From Vaison, a hundred towns, villages and monuments beckon to us, and what could be more enjoyable than to zigzag from one to the other. The best way is to come upon them suddenly and find ourselves unexpectedly greeted by the most pleasant surprises. To do so, we must centre our excursion around Mont-Ventoux, that lofty, wooded promontory some six thousand three hundred feet high, whose peak affords a superb panorama of the entire countryside.

Climbing Mont-Ventoux is always a magnificent experience, from wherever we start. The most usual starting point is the north slope, in imitation of Petrarch who was the first one known to have scaled these heights. "For many years now have I thought of making this excursion," he said. "Since my childhood this, by the grace of the power which governs man's fate, has been my place of abode, this mountain which can be seen from afar on all sides and is almost constantly before my eyes. An irresistible

urge overtook me to make that climb, once and for all, which I have so often made in my fancy." Let yourself be tempted as Petrarch was and you will return enchanted.

Millions of tourists, in imitation of Petrarch, have made this climb—now less difficult to do—up the north slope by way of Malaucène, Le Groseau and Mont-Serein. The south slope includes Bédoin, Saint-Estève, Sainte-Colombe, Le Chalet Reynard and La Grave. It passes first through bright sunshine, then through dark forests; and the east slope takes us through Sault, blue with lavender, and the little village of Le Ventouret, beyond which we find only naked gravel where trees can no longer grow and only aromatic grasses can keep a foothold.

Whatever slope is chosen, we are faced with a variety of vistas at each step of the way. But at the very top the wonder of wonders awaits. The plain, at our feet, stretches far and wide for almost two hundred miles all around and is cut off by the sky alone. This plain is a tapestry embroidered with woods, rocks, towns, villages, and flowing waters rushing towards the edge of the circle. From the top, to the north, the same great Alps we saw, from the Dauphiné and Savoy, among which the peaks of

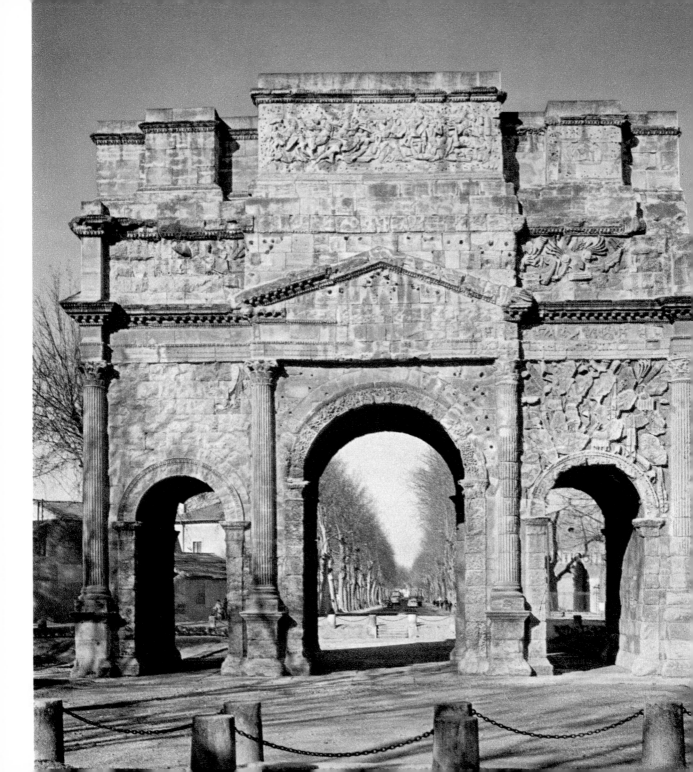

Ecrins, Le Pelvoux and Belledone and snow-capped Mont Blanc stand out. Turning to the east, at the foot of the Alpes-Maritimes, we can trace with our eye the line of the sea all the way from the Italian border, over L'Estérel and Les Maures, to the Cap de Creux and the Spanish border; to the west lies Le Canigou, and the dark and spiny Cévennes mountains are discernible with the peaks of Saint-Loup and Aigoual rising above the rest. Before them glimmers the Rhone, open to receive the waters of the Durance. The winding, undulating Drac is visible as it flows through the Provence of the Rhone, weaving through Avignon, Tarascon, Beaucaire, Arles and so many other towns and villages glittering in the sun or faintly visible under a pall of clouds. Our view embraces all, each town and village we passed through, in an all-inclusive composite. Marseilles shines through the faint mists. Saintes-Maries-de-la-Mer appears as a series of golden dots farther on. With nightfall come the revolving lights which trace the coastline from the isles of Marseilles to Sète—multi-coloured flashes which only add to the dreaminess of the twinkling stars. The panorama before us encompasses departments or, even more important,

WALL OF THE THEATRE • 12 ►

an entire country: our destination—le Comtat, the great Provence of olden times, land of the Count-kings of Boson and Forcalquier—a vast homogeneous country.

The countryside reveals all this land has suffered, desired, and loved: the chaos after the Flood, the mountain chains which suddenly rose up, crumbled and fell until the final mould was shaped, the Rhone and its branches born. Souvenirs both natural and man-made attesting to these origins have been preserved and move us with the depth of their meaning. Prehistoric man, the Iberians and the Ligurians, the Greeks and the Romans, the Barbarians, the Moors, frantic devastators and those who merely chopped down the woods to feed their fires, have left their mark on this select province. At Cabrières, at Oppède, to name only two, religious wars added to these ruins; at Lacoste, Bédoin and elsewhere, the Revolution left its own marks. Although the hue and cry was no doubt often raised in these belfries, they would more often resound over the valley of the Vaucluse, that blue line in the mother-of-pearl of the cliff, to announce a festival; here, too, Petrarch, whose faith and wisdom inspired many a troubadour, sang of his love.

But let us now return to the Comtat Venaissin and the wealth of surprises it holds in store for us.

From Carpentras, an eclectic route passes through Pernes-les-Fontaines, Saint-Didier with its generous waters, La Roque-sur-Pernes, tiny Beaucet, Saint-Gens, twice a year the scene of well-attended pilgrimages, Vénasque with its beautiful Roman church, Méthamis sitting atop its rock and surrounded by mountains, land of hunters and colliers; next we pass through lavender-scented Javon, Sault, Villes-sur-Auzon, Mazan and the many Gallo-Roman sarcophagi in its beautiful cemetery. From there, to close the circle, we return to Carpentras.

Apt is another high point of our trip, with its many sights, especially the cathedral of Sainte-Anne. From Apt we continue on to Thor to admire its beautiful Roman church and see the vines of chasselas grapes, then on to the green waters of Isle-sur-Sorgue, to the Fountain of the Vaucluse of Petrarch and his Laura, to proudly perched Gordes and the neighbouring Cistercian abbey of Sénanque still inhabited by monks clad in white, then to Roussillon with its many-hued ochre earth, until we return through rich orchards to Apt, where these same fruits are preserved.

17

▲ 14 • NOTRE-DAME D'AUBUNE

▲ 15 • CLOISTER OF THE ABBEY OF SÉNANQUE

• GORDES

• THE ROMAN BRIDGE AT MANE

The majestic Mont-Ventoux serves as a backdrop for the noble plain of Orange, turned to dust under the unrelenting sun. The Triumphal Arch welcomes guests arriving by road; those arriving by the river will pass it and the amazing Roman theatre. The pearly sky dips and rises around the towers and crenellations of Montfaucon; Caderousse lies huddled, enclosed within its ramparts. And, with the increasing brightness of the country-side, life itself increases in joy. Château-neuf-du-Pape rises above its elongated peak, its old donjon borne on thick waves of vine. A smile comes over us as we remember the story of the Pope's mule, for Avignon is not far off.

And soon it appears, a copper-coloured mirage. If you have managed to arrive with the setting sun, a gasp of admiration will rise within as you see the lacy castle flanked by seven crenellated towers, one for each of the seven popes who celebrated mass here, traced against the silken sky. This is Avignon, dotted with innumerable belfries, where three hundred bells ring out in such beautiful harmony that it is known as the herald city of joy. It lies before us like a gleaming Jerusalem of the old prayer books. From its long history as a papal city, Avignon has retained its sense of grandeur and love of festivity. Mistral re-calls this in his epic Poem of the Rhone:

For Avignon, Saint-Peter's foster child
Who in her port has seen his ship arrive,
And hung upon her crenellated belt
His keys. . . . .
. . . .
And who, despite the glory now gone by,
Lives on completely nonchalant of all.

But let us go into the city and roam about its streets filled with wonderful sights and admirable mansions. We owe it to ourselves to see it all: the Palace of the Popes, of course, the nearby Rocher des Doms which commands a magnificent panorama embracing an unbelievable horizon which extends from the Dentelles de Montmirail to Lubéron and the Alpilles, over the flowering fields and fertile plain bordered by the Durance. Back in the city itself we must stop to admire the Petit Palais of the archbishops, the Hôtel de la Monnaie, visit the Calvet Museum, whose architecture is pure eighteenth century, with its collection of carved stone, the many churches and, finally, enjoy a stroll along the narrow streets to come out suddenly upon a little shaded square or before one of the many branches of the river Sorgues which is still used to crank the ancient wheels of the dyer.

20

◄ 19 • VILLENEUVE-LÈS-AVIGNON • HOSPICE MUSEUM • CROWNING OF THE VIRGIN (DETAIL) BY ENGUERRAND-CHARENTON (FIFTEENTH CENTURY)

20 • PAPAL PALACE • LIFE OF SAINT MARTIAL
▼ FRESCO BY MATTEO GIONANNI DE VITERBO (FOURTEENTH CENTURY)

VILLENEUVE-LÈS-AVIGNON SACRISTY OF THE FORMER COLLEGIATE • POLYCHROME IVORY STATUE OF THE VIRGIN • 21
▼

In the middle of the Rhone is the island of La Barthelasse, and on the other bank, once reserved for the King of France when the Popes ruled here, rises Villeneuve, the Versailles of Philip the Fair, whose tower and Fort of Saint-André still stand, with its thick baked earth walls, its gardens, its ancient mansions and its magnificent monastery. Between these two once rival towns stands the half-destroyed bridge, built by the shepherd Saint Bénézet and spanning the rushing Rhone, celebrated in song as the scene of dancing.

Not far from Avignon, at Barbentane, with its mitred tower built to exorcize evil spirits, the prancing Durance flows into the Rhone. On this same hill is the monastery of Saint-Michel-de-Frigolet whose bell tower can be seen from the river. It was here that the Reverend Father Gaucher, in Alphonse Daudet's story, damned his soul by making an elixir with the hillside herbs which scent the monastery. Immediately after, we arrive at Beaucaire on the banks of the Rhone. On one side is the ruined triangular donjon of the Montmorency castle, above a large festival ground; on the other is the well-restored manor-house where we can imagine the Roi René leaning out of the mullioned windows to admire the river as it continues in its course. In the foaming and watery caverns beneath the chateau lurks the river monster, La Tarasque, which, legend has it, Saint Martha overpowered and forced into hiding here.

From here we follow the road leading to the Pont du Gard, Uzès and Nîmes. No other road through this beautiful and rolling countryside of the Gard, once a part of the Languedoc and yet so Provençal in feeling, will serve to reveal all the magnificent things we have yet to see here: the three tiers of arches of the Pont du Gard, a superb example of the Roman art of building; the impressive Amphitheatre, Maison Carrée, Tour Magne in Nîmes, as well as the noble Louis XIV gardens around the Fountain; aristocratic Uzès with its unforgettable avenues, paths, harmonious vistas—it was of this place that Jean Racine wrote:

. . . And we have nights more beautiful than your days.

The rich plain, born of river deposits, fills with vines, corn, rice-fields, and we arrive in the country of Arles, the old capital city. This stubborn city which, as Mistral said, has been all a city can be, drowses now within its baked walls heavy with history, hugged between the two banks of the Rhone. This is the

beginning of the delta. The nearby sea once beat against the very ramparts of the city in the time of the Romans, to make of Arles a triple port, river, Sea and marsh, if a marsh may be said to have a port. A fleet of flat-bottomed animal skin boats wended their way through these half-sweet half-salt marsh lands which extended all the way to the imposing abbey of Montmajour and to the Alpilles, their port of call.

Arles and its surrounding area afford living proof of all the bygone ages: the obscure prehistoric times in the nearby Mountain of Cordes and the haunted plateau of Castellet; the time of the first Christians who were present when Christ Himself said mass at Les Alyscamps (and His knees made an impression on the stone); Les Alyscamps itself with its sarcophagi of all the great prelates and princes of the Rhone which were floated down the river to this sacred burial place. The city is enclosed by Roman ramparts; we may visit the excellently preserved Roman amphitheatre and theatre as well as the impressive underground Cryptoportiques, a part of the Forum, the Palais de la Trouille used by Constantine with its remains of well laid out Roman baths. The museums are rich in antiquities, both Christian and Gallo-Roman. The Hôtel de Ville, former palace of the ruling Roman *podestat*, is an excellent example of Romanesque architecture.

The kings of Arles were crowned in the cathedral of Saint Trophime, and it was here, too, that Frederick Barbarossa received the weighty crown of the Germanic Holy Roman Empire. But here, as in Avignon, we must visit the living city. The charming narrow streets with white-washed walls, the unexpected courtyards, those inner gardens where an occasional cypress leans in meditation and emits its odour of turpentine. These are the joys that await the wanderer who will meander through the town.

To know Arles, or rather the Arles country, completely, we must continue eastward to the stony deserted plain of La Crau, littered with millions of tons of pebbles and cut by green oases, and westwards to the lake-filled Camargue. These are different halves of a complete whole, with its violent contrasts which complement each other admirably around the city which is its heart.

To the west of the great Rhone, in this enormous triangle to which the river each year adds a million tons of alluvial land, extends the enchanted Camargue with its deserts, its moving dunes and salt flats, its marshes reflecting the lead-coloured sun, fleeting clouds, or gather-

ing storms, this is the resting place of millions of strange and rare birds. Avocets, egrets, herons of all colours, armadas of pink flamingoes and other water birds: ducks, marsh-hens, bitterns, gulls sport freely in the knowledge that this mysterious and antique land is their refuge, their inviolable sanctuary. The Camargue is the home of solitary souls: foresters, shepherds, fishermen, poachers, dreamers and gypsies. All live their strange existence outside the world in this vastness which the river ceaselessly renews, maltreats, pillages, upsets, destroys and constantly reshapes.

But let us continue our trip. The Rhone runs wanderingly through the plain, and idles among the endless rice fields. In places salt water plants, announcing that the Sea is not far off, take root and patch the earth, glinting here and there with spots of salt. Those who follow the river by road see this conflict between the river and Sea continue until, finally, the Sea wins out. For those who come by ship, the Rhone alone is master, black and heavy with alluvial soil, rippling with eddies and foam. How deep is the silence over this vast region. Clouds sailing through the sky reflect in the oily surface of the water. The solitude is absolute and even the ships we come upon cannot attenuate

▲ 25 • TAMBOURINE PLAYERS AND FARANDOLE DANC

▲ 26 • VILLENEUVE-LÈS-AVIGNON BY COROT

NT OF THE BRIDGE OF SAINT BENEZET

▲
27 • THE RHONE AND THE TOWER OF PHILIP THE FAIR

it. In the distance island after island attempts to rise from the waters—isles of dreams, from which hardly perceptible murmurs and chirpings reach us and tend rather to emphasize than break the silence.

A phantom town of white salt appears on the right bank. It is Salin-de-Giraud, a revolting agglomeration of factories when seen from the land side, but unreal and magical from the river. Although the Sea is still some ten miles off, a canal ushers its waters into Salin and deposits the gleaming pyramids of salt we see there. The very air is filled with its pungency and the muddy waters of the Rhone now fill with brine. Behind, as the river flows to meet the Sea, is the lagoon of Vaccarès. At night the lights from the coast inform you that the Mediterranean is not far. The ships glide through these brackish waters, through this land thrown up by the water itself, where life is killed by the salt. The earth is saturated with both and shimmers with puddles and salt crystals. The land moves apart as the river widens. The heavy mud comes together to form islands, moving sands, shelves, marshes, rivulets across a breadth of more than a mile and a quarter. All these waters and salt flats with their broken reflections make our heads spin. A small, pale

city preceded by a tower suddenly appears: Port-Saint-Louis. The closer we come, the more it seems to get smaller and sink into the water and salt white land. It is the river with the reversed and rippling image reflected in it that produces this false mirage, this seeming retreat, this fake grandeur. When we reach the city, sea-going vessels appear between the houses. To avoid the sandy estuary which continues for five more miles, a canal was dug from here to Fos-sur-Mer.

The immense river, meanwhile, slowly continues its solitary course. It flows calmly on towards the Sea, and once there clashes in wild and splendid fury. The indomitable Sea rebels against the invading river casting its sand and the fertile humus gathered along its course. The Sea puts up a strong resistance, sends forth its waves, and beaten, but still unconsenting, cries out shrilly. It is finished, and the river must give up its ripples and its name to combine its beauty with that of the Sea.

★

After our trip in the upper reaches—the Alps, Lure, Mont-Ventoux, the Lubérons—and, first above then along the capricious Durance, we are now back on the plain with its irrigation canals.

▲
31 • NIMES • THE FOUNTAIN GARDENS

◄ ▲
29 • THE AMPHITHEATRE

◄ 30 • THE MAISON CARRÉE

This is the rich country of fruits and vegetables, which spreads at the foot of the Alpilles from the ridge of Lamanon and which cuts into the blue chain extending from the Lubéron.

Although those who live in the mountain may disdainfully call this plain a mere cabbage patch, it is a singular place, moulded out of old humanity. Between the Durance of Orgon and the Rhone of Arles and Tarascon rises the limestone chain of the Alpilles which has watched over the battles and the passing parade of many civilizations. This blue mountain chain, child of the great Alps, cut off from the Lubéron, to the east, by the mad river, ends, to the west, at the edge of what was, over a long period, the giant delta of the river and is today the plain of alluvial land, rich with fields and vines, which extends from Tarascon to Arles. The Alpilles end here at the banks of these Roman waters, and the tower of the Caesars still rises above their final peak to watch over the canal of Marius. For it was from here, in the time of Marius, that ships left for Arles and Nîmes laden with building stone to be used for amphitheatres, theatres, embankments and ramparts. They would leave from Ernaginum (now known as Saint-Gabriel) and the stones would be transferred to flat-bottomed leather boats which carried them through the marshlands. In the rock, under the antique tower, we can still see one of the iron rings used for mooring these ships. A stele, erected by a widow on the death of her husband, naval chief of the station, was found here. When the waters receded, the town of Ernaginum died. It became a farming land and the new, soft earth was sown. A Christian hermit once lived and meditated under that tower which bore witness to the impermanence of temporal power. When the olive-trees replaced the flowing river forever blocked farther on, the great builders of the tenth century built the pure masterpiece, the superb church with its single nave which is still intact. Light enters the church through a round hole in its ceiling, guarded by two angels.

Let us trace the sun-filled Alpilles. First the south slope, a mineral replica of a lapis-lazuli sky, the hill shines with pebbles gilded by the sun and dancing in its rays. This mirage is known as the Old Dance, accompanied by the song of the crickets in summer. In winter, the mountains merely idle and drink in whatever sun their southern exposure affords them. Flowers grow in the protection of the rock, the more moving for their rarity; non-migratory birds sing

35 • SAINT-GILLES-DU-GARD • CENTRE PORTAL OF THE OL

◄ 34 • UZÈS • THE FENESTRELLE TOWER

F SAINT-MICHEL-DE-FRIGOLET • 33 ▲

CH

TARASCON • 36 ►

among the remaining foliage. Towns rise up on the peaks. After Saint-Gabriel, comes Mont-Paon, a perpendicular cone-shaped peak ending in a gazebo laid out like a Roman camp, which still bears the ruins of a Celtic dwelling place, hidden among the black-green pines, remains of an old Gallic forest. Descending towards the plain is the village of Fontvieille-aux-Moulins. The castle ruins at Font-vieille, protected on one side by the sheer slope of the Crau, which runs along the Alpilles, is accessible from three sides on the hilly north slope. A double wall surrounds it, part Roman and part Saracen, protecting the entrance. When it was built and by whom remains a mystery. At present, the lonely winds, the tawny-owl, the eagle-owl haunt the solitary plateau. But traces of all its occupants are visible and the ground gives forth debris of all the ages: Celtic, Gallo-Roman, and, above all, Moorish. The medieval fortress was built on the ruins of the Roman camp; remains of the apse of a chapel and a monastery or hermitage can be seen. In this isolation, as in Saint-Gabriel, the god of all solitude takes on his true dimension.

The east slope of Mont-Paon is famous for its proud aspect whose jagged arabesques cut into the sky. Here we find the town of Les Baux. We shall climb towards this land of proud barons, often victorious rivals over the Count-kings of Arles and of Provence, which is now but a poor village. The climb takes us through successive folds of bony olive trees which bend and dip in the perpetual wind, past groves and wild flowers, lone cypresses and gurgling streams. Above us, the city twinkles like a blue and white mirage roosted as it is on its perpendicular plateau, and seems both uninhabited and uninhabitable. A few more steps and all changes. The route changes its rhythm. Before us opens a great circle composed of other circles within it caused by the erosive action of the wind. These circles, one above the other, gave Dante the idea for his Inferno. In the naked wall of this bright Inferno strange shapes of monsters, stone dragons, eagles with outspread wings, grimacing Cerberuses, screech-owls, unmoving sphinxes and many other forms appear. Grottos cut into the bodies and heads of these monsters have yielded up bones, pottery, coins of our many ancestors and revealed the different civilizations that settled in these hills. A small coin, inscribed with the Greek of Mont-Paon, was found clutched in the bony remains of a hand here. This coin, inscribed with the name of this small Alpilles village, was all he carried across that temporal river of

41

▲
39 • GIPSY PILGRIMAGE

◀ 38 • LES SAINTES-MARIES-DE-LA-MER

40 • HORSEMEN OF THE CAMARGUE
▼

forgetfulness, his own river Styx, the Rhone.

Scaling, crossing, climbing the circles around the spur on which Les Baux is perched, we pass through many centuries of civilization. We find cave dwellings with black traces left by the smoke of their inhabitants, a ring cut directly into the rock of the ceiling from which, no doubt, a light was suspended; Roman remains known as the Tremaïe on which are engravings relating that Marius, Julia his wife and Martha the Salien, his inseparable prophetess, lived here; and the other rock, known as the Gaïes, adorned with broken busts, illegible characters and Greek palm-trees. Elsewhere, in the vale of La Fontaine, at the edge of an enclosed orchard, is the charming Pavilion of Queen Jeanne; above it, in the limestone block which closes the vale, the labyrinth of caverns becomes deeper and more confused: the Trou des Fées, the sorcerers' meeting place which is supposed to end in the sword-shaped grotto of Cordes dug by the Moors near Montmajour-d'Arles. Finally we reach the goat path, trod by the Celts, then by the Romans and all the other inhabitants, which leads to the village itself. From its upper reaches it taunts you with its gaping ruins, their wide Renaissance windows open to the sky, the elements, and the emptiness. The ruins are in a state of confusion, with the various centuries overlapping and vying with each other. The six-pointed star of Bethlehem used in the coat-of-arms of Les Baux symbolizes the claim of the princes of Les Baux that they were descendants of Balthazar, one of the Wise Men of the East. This star, which once stood over the city, can now only shine for us in our mind's eye.

From the height of the towers whose building spanned the centuries and whose walls and steps are made of giant blocks of stone, from the ends of the terraces, from the humble clock-tower and the pod-shaped promontory on which the village is perched, we have a commanding view of the entire country of Arles laid out at our feet: to the north we see the Alpilles; far to the east we can make out Mont-Ventoux and the mountains of the Vaucluse and the Lubéron; to the south are Mont-Sainte-Victoire and the gleaming Sea in the golf of Fos, and, close by, spreading throughout the south, La Crau which connects the Rhone and the Sea. Between the pebbled vastness and this gazebo, behind the frothing folds of the hillside, the cultivated valley, dotted with marshes and lagoons and gracious little villages patched with red and green, offer a restful sight to our amazed

THE ARLÉSIENNE BY VAN GOGH • 41 ▶

• RICE FIELD IN THE CAMARGUE

riz

• PINK FLAMINGOES ON THE LAGOON OF VACCARÈS

eyes. Arles, in the background of Mont-Paon and Montmajour, with its ribbon-like Rhone, appears as a shimmering mirage of light. Beyond this, we see the Vaccarès reflecting the sky, the broad Camargue asleep among its waters, until we come to that stone flower, the fortress church of Saintes-Maries-de-la-Mer; further on we can trace the ramparts of Aigues-Mortes.

• BULLS AND HORSES ON THE PLAIN IN THE CAMARGUE

On one of the next peaks, Aureille, culminating point of the Roman Aurelian Way, stands with its remains of a thirteenth century castle and magnificent houses fallen to rubble. Above Eyguières rises Roquemartine, a citadel built by titans and reduced by time and man. In this once heroic place, our climb takes us through oak and pine groves, by prairies of asphodels where, as in Les Baux, only lonely shepherds haunt these heights once filled with glory. The conquerors are gone forever, but the herds still pass over the thyme and lavender covered paths and have become one with the countryside.

Eyguières with its beautiful houses and limpid fountains is the centre of this pastoral land. Under the last of the eastern abutments of the Alpilles, facing south, Lamanon huddles, separated from the Trévaresse mountain chain of Aix by a mountain pass which was once the bed of a branch of the Durance river and is now used for irrigation canals.

In the flanks of the hill of Lamanon are the grottos of Callès. They were inhabited, uninterruptedly, from neolithic times to the eighteenth century. It was undoubtedly an important Saracen outpost. The mark left by the beams of a horse shelter in the tender rock appear as if they were made only yesterday. It served as a refuge for Protestants during the time of the religious wars. These grottos, as they now appear, form a true village in a hollow. The crumbly zaffre stone was cut into a maze of seats, cupboards, nooks and crannies which leads back to itself at different levels. The little cell-like dwellings built one above the other open up suddenly onto a magnificent vista. At the eastern end is Orgon, surrounded by the blue Durance, with its ramparts, its church, its groups of houses and its chateau of the Guise family nestled amid water-willows, birch-trees and changing sands.

We shall follow the river over the section between Lubéron and the Alpilles and then take the north slope of these mountains. This brings us first to Eygalières, the Assisi of Provence, with its rocks, pink flowering thyme and windy dawns rising among the cypresses. To the west, amidst a countryside admirable in its proportions and harmony, opens the Aurelian Way which leads from Aureille on the other flank, across the pass and follows the mountains to Arles and thence onwards to Rome. It passes by Romanin first, the once lordly domain which is now no more than a heap of ruins, dating back in part to prehistoric times. It was inhabited until fairly recently. Its Romanesque chapel was erected

Course de tave

BULLFIGHT

on the ruins of an ancient temple, and its bare-walled donjon of the Castle of Gantelmi once resounded with the song of many a troubadour—Bertrand de Born, d'Alamanon, Geoffroy Rudel—and saw Petrarch and his Laura of Noves.

And the Aurelian Way continues on. Soon, in the distance, Mont-Gaussier, known as the Lion of Arles, rises up. Van Gogh often painted it when he was in the asylum at Saint-Paul-de-Mausole. Frédéric Mistral sang of it in verse as beautiful as its rock.

Under this lion of rock which sings a shrill or gentle song in the winds of Provence, with which the pines and the crickets join in, huddles Saint-Rémy, made up of many towns: the present one, a composite of all those which preceded it, extends a warm greeting. It welcomes strangers, passers-by, the curious, and when this warmth is returned, it immediately opens its doors, offers its fire, its wine, its friendship. And how could we help but show an interest in this town surrounded here and there by its old ramparts, with its charming little Renaissance square and beautiful Mistral-Mondragon and Sade mansions, now turned into museums to house the wealth of Greek and Gallo-Roman sculpture treasures of the region. The oldest existing Saint-Rémy, the one which was built closest to the mountains, is the most glorious. Patient and wise digging are bringing to light this nearby Pompei with Marius's triumphal arch and the beautiful mausoleum of Julius—a Roman city slowly emerging from the earth. Beneath this is the older Greek city, and beneath that the Ligurian; still deeper, the nameless prehistoric city. These three or four towns built one on top of the other were built among orchards of century old olive-trees growing out of the golden sands deposited here by ravines. Not far were—are still—the quarries which provided those hard stones the Romans used to build their most superb and eternal monuments. Next to the main and true underground town, the eleventh and twelfth centuries built the convent known as Saint-Paul-de-Mausole with its pure Roman cloister and magnificent belltower, covered in stone slabs, where Van Gogh stayed for a year after leaving Arles, before going to Auvers where he killed himself. During the First World War, Dr. Albert Schweitzer was among the civilian prisoners from Alsace who were sent here and stayed for several months. His good works were known all over Saint-Rémy and he was made an honorary citizen of the town.

We shall stop here a while. This was the city known to the Romans as Glanum. Let us wander about and see the ancient remains where Nostradamus of Saint-Rémy often came to prophesy. Many a Roman Centuria speaks of this city as his home. Our fancy takes flight as we amble among the many nostalgic shadows, the vegetal silver-grey countryside tented by the blue sky and gilded with the life-giving pollen shed by the flowers, or aired by the morning dew of almond trees. Our view fixes on a Giottoesque scene or a subject for a Cézanne painting. Van Gogh, too, forever captured the calm and the turbulence of this country—the long, black-tongued cypresses bent by the mistral, the fields of sunflowers rotating like the sun in the sky. The very stones seem to rise and fall in the shimmer of the heat which sets the beat to a perfect rhythm. The god of the forests, his beard of tangled roots, rises from the Roman ruins to watch over the fruits and vegetables which irrigation waters help to grow. The denuded Alpilles stand in beauty ready to receive the poor or the artists seeking refuge. Its warm air and waterless earth dance and shine in a mirage born of the sun's rays.

As we continue our descent, we come upon Eyragues and its neighbour Châ-teaurenard crowded with tomatoes, aubergines, peaches: nearby Maillane extends a different welcome. It was here that Mistral, the Homer of Provence, was born, lived and died after having created his masterpieces for the world. His house, now turned into a museum, is filled with souvenirs of his life and invaded by his still throbbing soul. His shade invites us to step over the threshold and dream of immortal fruits, of the beauty we have sought after in this ramble and found in this moving and inspiring land of Provence where grace and sensitivity abound.

On the horizon, the small grey mountains gradually disappear: these are the mountains painted by Chabaud as Cagnes was by Renoir, the Alpilles by Seyssaud and Van Gogh, and Sainte-Victoire by Cézanne. In the direction of these hills flows the Rhone, below Frigolet, or rather more precisely, below Boulbon, the charming perched village with its ruined fortress still surrounded by high walls. Halfway up this hill is the great Roman church of Saint Marcellin. Each year a festival is held for men alone to celebrate the new wine, and each participant joins the procession with his own full bottle. Libations are drunk to a Christian replacement for the Bacchus of the ancients in thanksgiving for a

57

◄ 52 • THE FORTRESS OF LES BAUX-DE-PROVENCE   ▲
53 • PROVENÇAL CRIB

◄ 54 • PEASANT FIGURINES

generous harvest. The Church, adopting the pagan ceremony, replaced Bacchus by Saint Marcellin, patron saint of water and wine. The clergy carrying banners lead the procession in great pomp. Under the vault of the church, the ceremony, reserved of course only for men, consists of the ritual blessing of the bottles and each one drinks at the sign of the priest, while the trumpets blare forth. After the sermon, which is given in Provençal, toasts are proposed and glasses clinked at the main altar.

So much for the patron saint of the wine.

As for the patron saint of waters, this is the handsome, very dignified Roman Saint Christopher who, in the lower village, on the banks of what was once the great Rhone, carried the Infant Jesus across the river on his shoulders and turned his old face, wrinkled with age and care, towards Him.

And now we return to the river whose waters have guided us through this land of sun. See the ships carrying other voyagers over its rushing waters. We have completed the circle of the Rhone flowing towards this land to the Rhone which leaves it. But our visit to beautiful Provence is not yet at an end. For the Sea is still there before us and beckons us to its laughing, magical shores.

★

Now for another excursion, one of the most interesting: Apt and the Roman bridge of Julian, still intact, Moorish Saint-Saturnin-d'Apt, Lioux, Murs, the Haut-Lubéron and Sivergues overhanging an abyss, Buoux and its fortress, Lourmarin and its beautiful chateau, the Medici Villa of Provence.

Our tour of the Lubéron begins at Gordes. Our visit takes us to one after another of the places which became famous in the time of religious persecutions, scattered with ruins—and what ruins—Oppède-le-Vieux with its windswept, razed castle, Ménerbe standing like a ship's prow on the plain, Lacoste whose manor-house, detested house of the Marquis de Sade, was destroyed during the Revolution. The Route des Crêtes on the other side of the Lubéron, leads to Mérindol on the other slope.

We pass through harmonious Bonnieux, and from there a side road leads to the curious Roman edifice of Saint-Symphorien, to Buoux, to Agnels, and leads us back to Apt or to Cavaillon by way of La Combe de Lourmarin, Cadenet-sur-Durance, Lauris and Mérindol.

Cavaillon, although well-known as the melon capital, contains many an interesting sight: the cathedral of Saint-Véran and its cloister, a synagogue, a Roman triumphal arch, a museum, the Plateau

56 • ANTIQUE REMAINS IN SAINT-RÉMY-DE-PROVENCE • MAUSOLEUM AND TRIUMPHAL ARCH

57 • BAS-RELIEF ON THE MAUSOLEUM (DETAIL)

of Saint Jacques where the humble Roman chapel commands a dizzying vista over the Durance and across the rich plain, heavy with fruits, to the Alpilles.

We must not leave the banks of the Durance without going to Pertuis to make the rounds of the chateaux of the Lubéron. The beautiful road from Aix to Pertuis passes Cadenet and a detour leads us to the abbey of Sylvacane, to Cucuron, with its chateau, and the vast panorama from its church, its great gate turned into a bell-tower. We can visit the picturesque lagoon of nearby La Bonde. And now the chateau country begins: the chateau of Ansouis, part medieval and part Renaissance where we may see the bedchambers of Saint Elzéard and of Sainte Delphine of Sabran. The chateau ruins and terrace are an imposing sight and give onto a commanding panorama. We wend our way through orchards and soon reach Mirabeau, proud seventeenth century manor-house of the Mirabeau family, with its four perfectly preserved massive towers in the angles of its well-restored stone walls. A little to the right, spanning the Durance, is the old fortified bridge which guards the rough approach and leads us to the Romanesque chapel of Sainte-Madeleine, the fifth century chapel

of Saint Eucher built against the cliff, Saint Eucher's grotto, and finally the feudal castle of Cadarache, the last stop on this tour. The road now returns to Pertuis, Aix or Avignon.

There is yet another wonderful excursion we can take: the Lavender circuit. It is to Carpentras that we owe the idea for this excursion, for although we may start from Avignon (and pass through Bonpas to see the famous monastery), it is from Carpentras that we enter upon the grey-green, grey-violet sea whose subtle scent drunkens the spirit. Our aim is Haute-Provence. Few regions are as grandiose in their noble sobriety, few cities and villages have managed to keep their character so well. Leave Avignon or Carpentras and from either go directly to Mont-Ventoux, which we climb by way of Bédoin and descend by way of Sault, Revest-du-Bion, Banon, Saint-Etienne-les-Orgues, Forcalquier, old capital of the Count-kings, Manosque-des-Plateaux, Gréoux-les-Bains (by a detour well worth the time), the plateau of Valensole, Riez, Moustiers-Sainte-Marie on its cone-shaped hill with its symbol of the star. From there we continue our descent, but this time in the direction of the Sea, and for this we take a new kind of road—a truant's road. The mountain chains appear in a different

65

◀ 59 • THE CHATEAU OF LOURMARIN   ▲ 60 • THE ALPILLES

◀ 61 • A FOUNTAIN IN SALON-DE-PROVENCE

light, the lavender fields and the woods present a new aspect. Here we come upon the magnificent *corniche*, the wild gorges of the Verdon, so justly famous, Comps, the Plan-de-Canjuers still haunted by the legendary character of Mélusine. Soon we arrive at old Castellane-en-Montagne where the Route Napoléon, leading to Grasse, the perfume city, starts.

For if we continue our descent from here towards the Sea, the primordial Sea which, from near or far, makes its mark and creates its special colour, we shall see the varied flora of Provence turn slowly into that of Africa. Mimosa, eucalyptus, cultivated flowers, uncultivated scented trees indicate that the Riviera is near, that well-named land of sun and foaming Sea from whose waters Aphrodite, goddess of these regions, is daily reborn in Greek legend.

★

But let us not go to the Sea just yet. Let us linger yet a while in this hinterland from which the history of the land itself and of man is descended.

Haute-Provence! The cool magic of this name. What more fitting description than that given by one of her own sons, Alexandre Arnoux in his *Géographie*

Sentimentale: "I call Haute-Provence that land of fancy, of mirages and of penury, leaning against a rampart of olive-trees, with its terraces of crude rock and poor yield, its fields of lavender, thyme and rosemary, richer in scent than gold, this land crawling between mountain peaks where the chamois and the he-goat live, the prairies of gentians and the orchards of the Var, the land of Aix and of Avignon, between the alpine pasture lands and the realm of Arles, between the high-rising peaks of the Trois-Evêchés and the Pelat, and the rose fields of Grasse. . . . I call Haute-Provence this solitary land of lavender fields and cold sun, the middling river Durance and its hinterlands to the east, inextricable, mountainous, which becomes entangled and moves towards the glacial fields huddling together to the east, last boundary of the Mediterranean land, there where the olive-tree no longer grows and only the light replaces it."

We can take the road through Vérignon and the Plan-de-Canjuers—the first towns we encounter, bewitching sights. In the summer this route is bordered by flowering lavender: Aiguines and its old Roman bridge, the gorges of the Verdon with its canyons and chasms, and, at the end of this climb, Moustiers-Sainte-Marie where, suspended from its

chain hung between two peaks, shines the star of Les Blacas which a knight forged, so the legend claims, from his prison irons when he escaped out of slavery from the Moors. Moustiers is another Bethlehem, but a Bethlehem of the hills under a pure sky and has remained such: simple and pure. When, in the starry night, the walls shine dotted with trembling lights, the mountain seems to rise mystically to the stable, the humble Manger of the Nativity.

I have not forgotten Castellane, cut into the side of a rock, nor Riez with its four Roman columns arising from a field. Castellane-Riez, Castellane-Moustiers are two routes which lead to the very heart of Haute-Provence.

Moustiers to Manosque. This route crosses the wide plateau of Valensole, that sea of lavender under the fast moving clouds pushed along by autumn winds. The almond-trees in winter, black and naked, gesticulate in the wind. In the spring they are covered with thousands of white and pink blossoms of a grace indescribable in words and uncapturable even in water colours.

Then we reach Manosque, the city of the plateau which Giono describes so well, rich in history, opening on to a vast yet soft panorama. This old country has been the site of many varied civili-

zations, was plundered, yet, obstinate for life, has continued on. It is the land of winds and a mountain pass, called the Col de Toutes Aures, was named for them. The ceramists of Moustiers, heirs to the great pottery tradition of bygone days, piously mould, shape, bake and love the little statues of Notre-Dame-des-Vents for which they are known. Many a house and many a poet have reserved an oratory or a nook for them, be it on the wall or in the hollow of their hearts.

All the surrounding villages, in the gruff shadow of the great mounts of Lure, reflect the balminess of the weather. To pass through is exquisite; to live here would be very demanding in many ways, for they have maintained a life made up only of bare essentials and have not yet become blasé and worldly. Feudal Pierrevert, Montfurron with its old unworked mill rising in the background like a Primitive painting; Sénès the episcopal; Barrème and Mézel; Lincel where so many witches were burnt; Saint-Martin-l'Eau; Puimichel tumbling down from its high-perched, ruined donjon; Entrevennes with its splendid remains now poor but proud: everywhere we see remains of grandeur, a renunciation, an acceptance of the inevitability of change. Baumugnes, Aubignane and

▲
68 • LA CRAU D'ARLES BY VAN GOGH

▲
◄ 66 • LAVENDER FIELD NEAR VALENSOLE

◄ 67 • VINEYARDS AT VERDIÈRE

those many villages which Giono calls the villages of care in the silence of the mountain; Montjustin, Redortiers, Le Comtadour are the most moving. The nearby Lure sounds the keynote of vastness and starkness for the entire region.

Forcalquier still appears as a wasps nest around its citadel; this is the first capital of the ancient ruling family of the Bérengers. The four daughters of Raymond Bérenger, all of whom became queens, were born here. The eldest of them, Marguerite of Provence, married the young Louis IX, the future Saint Louis, and was thus instrumental in uniting independent Provence with the kingdom of France, so desirous of extending its boundaries.

To the west of the city, past Mane and Porchères, the dome of Saint-Michel-l'Observatoire, the largest in Europe, shines under a pure sky, the purest in all France, and has therefore become an important scientific station.

We continue from Forcalquier by way of Cruis, Fontienne, Saint-Etienne-les-Orgues on the route used to take the flocks to mountain pastures until we arrive at the foot of the Lure mountains, which Giono called the monstrous spine of the bulls of Dionysus, and which

stand out as a series of great ships, one behind the other, sailing on a rocky sea, their prows rising proudly to defy the vast emptiness before them. On one of these mountains is the ancient hermitage of Saint-Donat and the small pilgrims' church of Notre-Dame-de-Lure ; on another, the convent of Ganagobie, with its beautiful apses and deserted ruins, and, on the same mountain just about three miles distant by a forest path, the village of Lurs hangs over the vast rolling and pebbly Durance; village of the Templars and of the Renaissance, land of neglect which may some day be reborn. Close by are the Mées mountains and their procession of petrified monks in descent. And if we follow this ever mounting path we shall finally arrive at the extreme edge of Provence. To the north, from its pine covered slope, Sisteron, the old town with its imposing citadel atop its rocky base at the edge of the mad Durance, overlooks the Dauphiné, and from the south slope the rich, sun-filled, golden plain where the first olive-trees sway in the breeze. This is the Provence of the poet Paul Arène, who sang its praises.

I like to approach Aix from these light-filled mountains. For Aix, although it is so close to the Sea, huddled within this circle of mountains, is the heart of

CARYATID ON THE PAV

THE CATHEDRAL OF SA
ON THE MAIN PORTAL (S

STATUE FROM THE CHAT

▲
74 • THE PAVILION OF V

▲
75 • THE FONTAINE DES QUATRE-DAUPHINS

▲
76 • THE CLOISTER OF SAINT-SAUVEUR
(TWELFTH CENTURY)

this country, even if many of the peaks are only of middling height—except for Mont Sainte-Victoire, or, as it is known in Provençal, Ventùri, Mount of the winds. Like all mountain cities, Aix is enclosed within itself; like them, too, it is covered with light mists which rise up from its sparse waters, its Arch and its many fountains.

The wealth of Aix has come down through all the ages. Its Roman remains, its still popular thermal baths, suffice to prove its ever-lasting importance. The Count-kings of independent Provence had made Aix their capital during the Middle Ages, for they too felt that this city, in the shape of a half-opened rose, was closer to the Alps of Forcalquier than to the Mediterranean of Marseilles or the Rhone of Arles. Strange destiny for a southern city to be considered part of the mountains.

During the seventeenth century, Aix was at its height of perfection. It was the seat of the Etats and of the Parliament, and all the great names of the day spent some time here. It was a very ceremonious time, and Aix retained as a souvenir of these years of glory the splendid residences, now decaying with age, the sign of their nobility and, therefore proud of their very decrepitude. At every step of the way, in each old ceremonious street, on the Cours Mirabeau, peaceful domain of the Roi René, we find sculptured gateways, caryatids by the hand of Puget supporting balconies and wrought iron balustrades. The famous cathedral of Saint-Sauveur is sculptured and adorned like a shrine, a fit home for the admirable triptych of Nicholas Froment: the *Burning Bush*. The museum and libraries of Aix are famous, too. Nothing is lacking in this city: archeology, painting, sculpture, earthenware, furniture, tapestry, souvenirs of tradition and of folklore. Music is queen here, too, for Aix has become another Salzburg, where each year in July music lovers come from all over Europe. Unfortunately, modernism is taking a great foothold here daily, and the beautiful old city, standing in the way of progress, is slowly falling under the impact of the bulldozer; porphyry columns are being razed to the ground and the precious mosaics of the emperors are being covered over by cement. Sainte-Victoire, the pagan mountain immortalized by Cézanne, the Provençal Sant Ventùri, even, is in danger at the hands of these new builders who are now beginning to invade the skyline of which it once was sole master. What would a new Cézanne do faced with this sacrilege? Visit Aix before it is too late.

LES MARTIGUES • 7

Armand Vernier

THE BRIDGE OF FLAVIAN (FIRST CENTURY) • 7

THE ÉTANG DE BERRE • 8

See it and feel it. Listen to the weeping fountains and the great and merry operas of Mozart.

★

The Mediterranean Provence begins, naturally enough, at the manifold delta of the Rhone. It therefore includes, as we have seen, the strange land of the Camargue made of alluvial deposits, continually deepened and enlarged, constantly changed and remoulded. Despite the constant flow of tourists which crowd this land of salt and water more than any other, when seen at the right time of year the Camargue still appears unsullied. Under the great autumn and winter skies it once again becomes a stopping off place for migrating birds, a land of vastness, solitude, and mirages invaded by wild horses and bulls, a camping ground of saints and aloof gypsies. What a pity that the great religious pilgrimages today turn into the most vulgar of fairs. Could they but see it now, would the Apostles once again anchor their boats along these shores?

The maritime Provence begins here, in the creeks, coves, ports, bright with life-giving sun, and stretches all the way to where the snow-covered Alps of Peira-Cava mingle with wild boundary waters.

Let us follow this enchanted coast. The great branch of the Rhone (the only navigable one) has just ended at Port-Saint-Louis-du-Rhône, at the extreme tip of the Golfe de Fos where Port-de-Bouc bustles with fishermen and shop-keepers. Port-de-Bouc is the seaside of Les Martigues which—often called the Provençal Venice—is the gateway to the Etang de Berre which is now an enormous refinery port. It is difficult to imagine that this was where the first Greeks landed, well before those who were to found Massalia. The only remains left to us of this Greek migration is old Saint-Blaise perched on its high, cliff-like plateau, which archeological diggings have been restoring to its old former shape. Not so very long ago Maurras was to write of Saint-Blaise: "we occupy the last balcony from which we may look out onto the whole maritime marshland of the lower countryside. From here the inland sea of Berre opens out like a pink chalice. The elongated surface of Caronte joins it, in the distance, with the purple Sea beyond which runs the Rhone, a black dragon, opaque and impenetrable even to the evening light." What would he say of it now. Its refineries kill the fish in the lagoon and blacken the sky with smoke and diabolical constructions.

But let us continue our trip. We come to Carro, Cap Couronne and its village, the remains of the watch-tower once

MARSEILLES • THE VALLON DES AUFFES • 82 ▲

▲
" PÉTANQUE " PLAYERS • 83 ►

" APÉRITIF " TIME • 84 ►

A STREET IN OLD MARSEILLES • 85 ►

used to warn the people of the arrival of pirates. Each cove has now become a resort village in the sun, overrun with villas. Sausset-les-Pins, Carry-le-Rouet and Le Rove huddle comfortably or hide from the sea breeze, L'Estague, an outer harbour of Marseilles, whose town and port are both abustle. Out on the Sea gleam islands, and over the heavy-laden waves, high in the sky, stands the Virgin of the Garde—Notre-Dame-du-Bon-Voyage—who follows sailors far out to sea and is the first to greet them upon their return.

And now the two curves of the bank come harmoniously together, the one going out to the Rhone which gently fills it with sand and, to the east, the other, rocky bank with its small ports which serve as extensions of the harbour of Marseilles. One side is sheltered and the other leads out to the open Sea. The port and endless embankments are a beehive of activity. This is undoubtedly the heart of the Mediterranean, choice spot for a great city, universal cross-roads. It is a pure and deep harbour, well protected from the gusts of the mistral and easily navigable despite the hills which appear on the horizon. The Sea and the nearby Rhone open the world to the north and to the south. Marseilles stands perpetually offering her vast blue waters to all the shores they touch, to these brown-skinned men they rather join together than separate. Maurras wrote: "this is where the nuptial altar of the Greeks and the Gauls was raised, and the great civilizing wedding consummated."

It has often been said that Marseilles is a melting pot where all races join together, that it is more a Mediterranean port than a large Provençal city. Yet, follow its coast, the famous *corniche* which marks the beginning of the Riviera, rich with palm and eucalyptus trees, past the picturesque coves of Vallon de L'Oriol and Vallon des Auffes, small fishing villages; these are true little villages, almost totally ignorant of their gigantic city, busy playing *boules*, caulking their meagre docks, weaving fishing nets in the sun, idling in the cafés, preparing a *bouillabaisse*. Everyone knows everyone else, addresses each other in the familiar form, jokes, speaks in Provençal—or French with a Marseillais accent. The happy times recounted in legends are still alive here. How pleasant to be able to mingle with these happy people and, as Suarès says, taste the Mediterranean in a cup-full of sun.

Let us now continue our tour along the capricious shore. We see the gleaming Marseilles-Veyre mountain chain reflected

principale base française
chantier de constructions navales

BORMES-LES-MIMOSAS • 87 ▲

SANARY • 88 ▲

was small fishing village touristo

in the rushing waters. The space is vast, solitary, grandiose, with its ancient forests, its sudden bends, its creeks hiding among bushes of rosemary play an eternal game of hide-and-seek. This is a beautiful trip filled with unexpected sights. The vista is ever-changing: Sea and island and hills around its edges. Soon the Sea is pushed back by the Caps Canaille and Soubeyran and cuts into the bay of Cassis, vast harbour some three miles long. In the upper regions, rising like a fort, is Le Gibal, home of the beautiful Estérelle, fairy-woman and heroine of the great poems *Calendal* and the *Baou Redoun (The Song of the Rhone)* of Frédéric Mistral. This is still known as Charlemagne's Crown. The view from these peaks, out onto the blue and emerald coves which zigzag along the coast, and magnificent coral reefs in the Sea is astounding. Of these coves, Pormiou and its neighbour the Cap Cacau which marks the tip of the bay, are notorious for their treachery and danger and are called, in memory of the Greek myth, the Scylla and Charybdis of Provence.

Cassis, famous for the vines waving on its slopes (vines imported from Sicily by the Roi René, who was particularly partial to this sweet muscatel), and La Ciotat, neighbouring city, renowned for its naval constructions, its quicklime, its cement and its industry, are each guarded over by ruined towers still rising on the peaks above them. These are the remains of watch-towers set up to warn the inhabitants of invasions, for this land was often raided and taken over by marauders. Proof of this is still to be seen in the remains of dead cities such as: Tauroentum, a Phoenician city first, then Greek, then Roman, and now completely covered over by sand, the village of La Cadière where survivors of these invasions sought refuge, and old La Ciotat: Citharista, the city of the zither which the Saracens destroyed along with so many other smaller ones.

Bandol, Sanary and Le Brusc were, until recently, simple fishing villages, and have now, with the increase in tourists, become hotel centres. Mimosa, eucalyptus and palm-trees with flowering parasitic creepers, begin to appear among the Provençal cypresses and olive-trees. This is the Riviera, which is not included in our ramble. The traffic, the rush of cars and bathers, half-dressed visitors taking in the sun, indicate that we are now come to the Mediterranean playground.

Between the two sheer rocks of Cap Sicié and picturesque Le Six-Fours, after crossing the naval yards of

92

◄ 93 • THE ABBEY AT LE

▲
94 • FRÉJUS • BULLFIGH

AMPHITHEATRE

Tamaris-sur-Mer and La Seyne, we approach Toulon, the great military port. This sheltered harbour is unique in the world. Coming upon this immense cove, huddled at the foot of a mountain protecting it, and extending over about a hundred and twenty-five miles, knocked against by waves at either end, we cannot stifle a gasp of admiration for this gulf guarding the sleeping city.

Its location combines all the requirements for a prosperous military and civilian city (with Saint-Mandrier as its enormous workroom), as well as a charming fishing port which it has always been. The small fishing craft dot the port among the great warships, and the sky of Provence smiles down on the city, undaunted by the smoke and the industrial uproar.

From time immemorial, Toulon has known how to put its natural advantages to good use. It was the preferred prey of the barbarians: Visigoths, Ostrogoths, Burgundians, Franks, Saracens. The latter were the most feared for their continual raids, and when they invaded they would set up in the ruins they had created and enslave the remaining survivors. William of Orange, called William the Short Nosed, Count of Provence, saved the country from these invaders, rallying the nobility, the knights and their people in a last victorious crusade. Toulon became French in 1481. Louis XII, Henry IV, Louis XIV, made of this the greatest port in France. Painting studios, sculpture studios were set up to decorate the magnificent ships, even the warships, and Puget and his followers came here to work. Figureheads and caryatids became fashionable and their use spread from Toulon throughout all of Provence. Marseilles and Aix still bear witness of this.

After having long been sited at Marseilles, the convict prison was transferred to Toulon. The beautiful terrace walls of dried stones, so useful for country hillside dwellings, are the work of the convicts thus employed while their ships were laid up in winter. They are still remembered in Toulon and many an old saying makes reference to them.

Napoleon and much later, at the Liberation of France, General de Lattre de Tassigny, freed Toulon from the hands of occupying armies. Of these memories, too, Toulon is both conscious and proud.

★

What is poetically known as the "Gay Kingdom of Provence" stretches much farther along the Sea until it reaches the Alpes-Maritimes, according to the laws

97

of geography—politically it included Nice when they were both ruled by the House of Savoy and was bounded by the Var river. Yet, for touristic reasons, the practice has been to include in the Riviera the entire coast from Toulon on. We must therefore respect, insofar as possible, this fashion and let ourselves be guided by it. Hyères still remains the flower of Provence, the light and soft Garden of the Hesperides which Hercules, in his wanderings, sought.

Off the coast of the city, scented with captivating perfumes and rocked by the swaying palms, the islands, justly called the Golden Islands, tempt the eye and instil a desire to linger and walk in the sun. We can best see these islands by a charming and pleasant boat ride. Rade de Giens, Tour Fondue, then Ribauds and Ribaudons, finally Porquerolles, called the island of Calypso, Port-Cros and the Ile du Levant. What a delectable feeling of adventure and solitude, under the giant eucalyptus-trees, if we take the trouble to arrive before or after the heavy summer invasion. Here we find the Lérins islands strung together like so many burnt amber and mother-of-pearl and gold beads in the sea. Francis I, art loving King, created the ephemeral marquisate of the Iles d'Or. How charming a title of nobility it made.

But let us continue on our trip along the coast. The granite arch extending from Les Embiez to Fréjus, the wild bank of Les Maures, undulates with its antique forests, dating back, geologically, to the time of the Flood, filled with cork oaks and chestnut-trees, majestic pines, mimosas, giant aloes, wild fig, orange, lemon, eucalyptus and palm-trees. It is a special land, living from the produce of its mountain, its hunts and its woods. The Moorish cities have retained their aspect, such as Bormes, scaling its flowery hillside, so covered with golden blooms that it is known as Bormes-les-Mimosas; after comes Collobrières with its fields of chestnut-trees and its forests of cork oaks, and, on the coast, Grimaud so beautifully located, and, above it, La Garde-Freinet, last of the remaining old haunts of the Saracens. Let us hope it will retain its Moorish aspect in its architecture and, above all, in its ramparts, its small streets, its ancient wells and its caverns in which provisions and firearms were stored. Back along the coast, surrounded by many minor resorts, we come upon Cavalaire and Saint-Tropez which has now become quite fashionable, Sainte-Maxime, Val d'Esquières, Saint-Aygulf, as much a paradise for bathers and summer holidayers as they once were resorts for comfort-loving, rich winter visitors whose great sunny centres still remain Cannes, Nice, Menton.

Connecting with the granite of Les Maures, the red volcanic Estérel descends from Mont-Vinaigre to the north and plunges into the Mediterranean in a multitude of flaming reefs and capes. Here we find, among others, Saint. Raphaël where the mistral is said to die-These coves, so overpopulated in the summer, taken together really make one long and narrow resort city running at the edge of a hinterland which has remained, by comparison, almost virgin and wild.

These narrow valleys, the interior vales of l'Estérel, and these grottos, have put up a fierce resistance throughout the ages. The Romans themselves could not subdue them. This is the preying ground of wild beasts and the home of rare flowers and, as a result, the favoured spot of hunters, scientists, geologists, and botanists, of artists and all those who seek solitude, as did the religious hermit saints of former times, be it to seek beauty or their secret soul or their God.

A little more inland we find Vallauris, the golden vale, with its ceramists, Biot, the home of glass-blowing, Grasse where, all the year, scent is distilled from flowers, and all the surrounding towns and high-perched villages: Tourettes,

Gourdon, Cabris, Bar-sur-Loup, Magagnosc, Thorenc and so many other tempting towns which invite us to stroll or make longer excursions. At Golfe Juan, Napoleon landed on his return from the Isle of Elba. This region, once deserted, this small composite of Africa, has become a true cosmopolitan meeting place.

As for Antibes where Paul Arène, one of the great Provençal poets, died, it is for me a religious place of poetry, for it was here that Arène, writing in the sun before his window, surrounded by his well-beloved clay figures, lost consciousness and his head fell among these tiny clay characters, similar to those still to be found throughout Provence. Those of Arène were placed with him in his coffin. They were of the same clay, our earth.

Cagnes-sur-Mer, land of Renoir. Cagnes-le-Vieux, a museum piece with its Middle Age corbellings and its magnificent countryside immortalized by the painter. Then Vence, the beautiful flowery town, and Saint-Paul, village of artists and antique dealers, these are the eastern boundary of old Provence. We shall soon arrive at the Var, the boundary line.

Is this then the end of our trip? Have we seen all there is to see in this glimpse of Provence? I rather think not, for the hinterland is perhaps the most personal still and has retained the most originality.

If we ascend from Vence, the eastern limit of the ancient county, we arrive at Bar, Tournon, Montauroux, Fayence with their valleys, their steep slopes, home of Gaspard de Besse, notorious bandit and valiant knight, then on to Seillans, wild and enchanting Valmasque, Bargemon, finally Draguignan, the chief city of these upper regions, with its House of Queen Jeanne and its Rock of Fairies, a dolmen shaded by the three sacred trees of the Celts as in bygone days: oak, African lotus, bent juniper. On the way out of Draguignan is the hermitage of Saint Hermentaire, celebrated for having exorcized these regions of a water monster which tormented them.

A bit farther on we arrive at the Cistercian abbey of Thoronet, an unadorned, severe masterpiece of the monastic art of the south. It is a world of stone gilded by the centuries and has been very well restored, although parts are still in ruins. The cloisters incite meditation, with their noble dimensions and lack of ornament, their columns adorned with strict measure, their Roman bays, the immensity of the interior which seems to be the very sculpture of space where the soul must find itself.

Brignoles, with its gentle climate, is not far. This was where the Countesses of Provence came to give birth. The old town has retained its charm and its atmosphere. At the foot of the modern city runs the Caramy, branch of the Argens. The atmosphere has an Italian limpidity brought about by the waters, the trees, the rocks shining and gilded with bauxite, and the orchards and cultivated fields scattered about with striking harmony. It is one of the many different Provences we meet which combines its temperateness with the light of the Sea, the vigours of the bitter mountains and wooded mountain chains. La Loube deserves a special visit, for from its peak we have an incredible, commanding panorama extending from the white Alps to Toulon, from Italy to Mont-Ventoux, from the forests of La Sainte-Baume to the brown shales of the Dauphiné.

At the foot of La Loube is La Celle, a restored abbey dating from the earliest Christian times, destroyed by the Saracens and rebuilt at the beginning of the twelfth century by the Count-Kings of Provence, the Raymond Bérengers. Garcende, Queen Mother, came here to take the veil, as did many daughters of the most illustrious Provençal families after her. The sarcophagus of Garcende, after the decadence and the ruin of the abbey, served as a trough for beasts. But La Celle has again been brought to life and today extends its luxurious hospitality.

Saint-Maximin, nearby, also possesses a great monastery under which, according to tradition, the first apostles are buried. Today, sepulchres and several tumble-down cottages rise among the ruins of the Roman town. This is the first Saint-Maximin. It grew up about its vast Gothic convent which warrants a visit. The magnificent pulpit of the eighteenth century relates the life of Mary Magdalene. Her tomb is at Sainte-Baume where she died after so many years of penitence.

By a delectable route, we continue from here to Barjols, the Tivoli of Provence, shelved on the flank of its refreshing hill, its forest murmurs mingling with the babbling of its brooks. Joseph d'Arbaud, the great French poet, is buried here, his harmonious soul rocked by harmonious nature.

★

Here our voyage comes to an end. We have wandered around the rose of Aix, that magnificent, magical flower asleep in the elegance and aroma of the bygone centuries. It is this scent which we take with us as a souvenir.

After having withstood the empassioned furors of the Rhone, filled our veins with the fruited air of the plain of the Durance, the pure and glacial air of the mountain peaks, that other golden purity of Mont-Ventoux and of Mont-Sainte-Victoire, and the sea breezes, it is only fitting to come to drift and dream in the harmonious air of a summer night in Aix, this enchanted stone chalice of a city.

We have seen and fondly admired all the famous sites, the monuments, milestones of all the past centuries. They fill us with a pride in the southern country and its ability to continue on through all the upheavals of the world.

Many civilizations have melted together, amalgamated insolubly to produce this Provençal race. It must be, as Lamartine proclaimed to Mistral, that there is a virtue in the sun. Its bright heat conquered the invaders and made them over into Provençaux. As an example of this, look carefully at the gigantic monument of La Turbie, this memorial built by Augustus. It bears, engraved on it, the names of all the tribes conquered by the emperor and subdued by him into submission to his rule. Undoubtedly they survive still, all of them, in us, and will continue to do so.

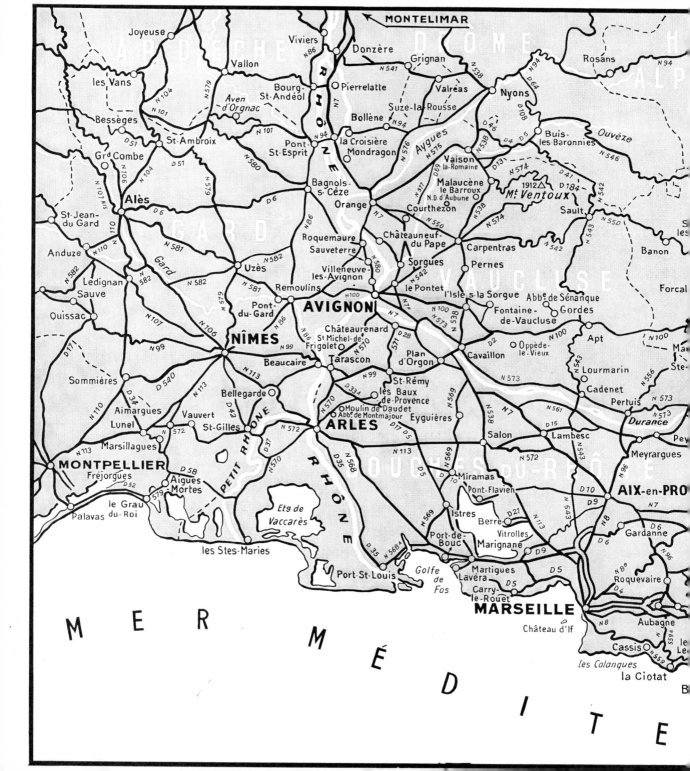

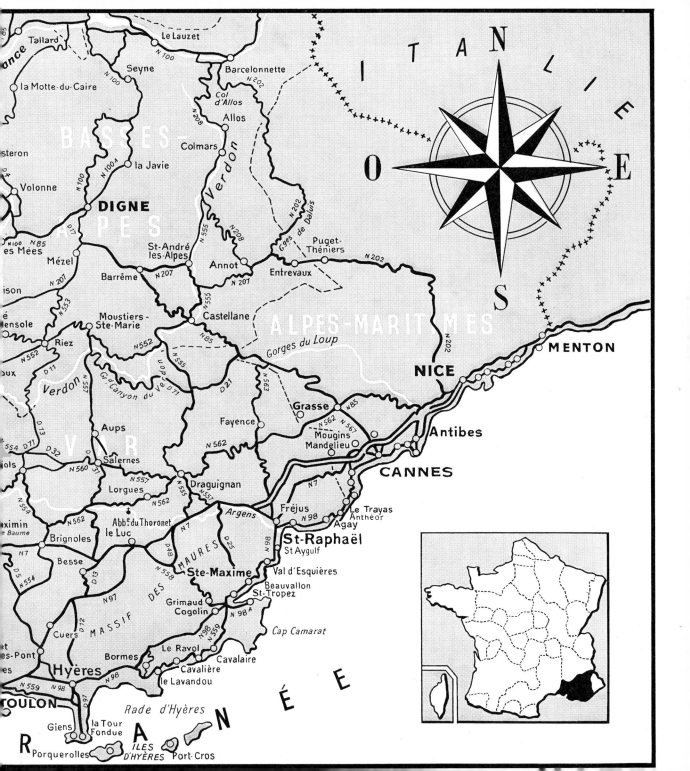

The photographs in this book are by : Georges Trubert (Nos. 2, 4, 5, 9, 10, 11, 16, 18, 27, 28, 31, 33, 34, 35, 37, 44, 45, 48, 51, 56, 60, 61, 64, 66, 67, 74, 75, 76, 79), Ervin Marton (Nos. 3, 15, 40, 49, 59, 88, 89, 92, 93, 94), Atziger (Nos. 1, 6, 7, 12, 13, 14, 21, 38, 52), Jacques Fronval (Nos. 22, 23, 32, 46, 55, 86, 87, 90, 91), Denis Brihat (Nos. 25, 39, 54, 63, 70, 80), Giraudon (Nos. 19, 20, 26, 41, 68, 69), Delmas (Nos. 8, 72, 73), Roland Gay (Nos. 17, 29, 58), Kammermann (Nos. 83, 84, 85), Machatschek (Nos. 50, 78, 81), Roger Perrin (Nos. 65, 82), Photo-Spirale (Nos. 36, 62), Pierre Tétrel (Nos. 30, 71), Doumic (No. 77), Féher (No. 47), Patrice Molinard (No. 53), Janine Niepce (No. 57), Actualit-Rapho (No. 42), Le Cuziat-Rapho (No. 43), Robert Thuiliers (No. 95), Yan (No. 24).

THIS BOOK WHICH IS THE EIGHTH IN THE SERIES PROSPECTS IN COLOR WAS PRINTED BY IMPRIMERIE CENTRALE LAUSANNE

FOR TUDOR PUBLISHING CO., NEW YORK